UNDER THE GROUND

Conceived and created
by Claude Delafosse
and Gallimard Jeunesse
Illustrated by
Daniel Moignot

HIDDEN WORLD

A FIRST DISCOVERY BOOK

SCHOLASTIC INC.

New York Toronto London Auckland Sydney

Under the ground
it is so dark that you
can't see anything.
This dark world
is an interesting place
to visit.

With this book, you will
be able to observe
animals that live
underground as though
you were there with them.

With a simple paper
flashlight, the world inside
the earth will be revealed
as you explore the pages
of this book.

Remove the paper flashlight from the back of the book.

The Rabbit
You may have already seen rabbits jumping around the countryside. But their homes are underground, where they are safe and warm and can raise their families.

Move the flashlight between the black pages and the plastic pages to discover hidden images.

If you go into the countryside
you can see lots of birds and horses,
butterflies and bees.
It might make you think
that all creatures
live above ground
all the time.

But there are
many, many creatures
hiding from you
underground.
Let's study them
with your
special flashlight.

The Rabbit

You may have already seen rabbits jumping around the countryside. But their homes are underground, where they are safe and warm and can raise their families.

The Mole

It is very rare to see this creature above ground. It is also hard to see the entrance to the complicated underground tunnels it digs with its strong, sharp claws. In these tunnels, the mole feeds on earthworms and insects, which it sniffs out with its highly sensitive nose.

The Earthworm

You probably have seen an earthworm above ground.
But earthworms usually travel through tunnels inside
the earth. An earthworm moves by contracting
and expanding its muscular body as it moves
forward. After a rain, worms often come above
ground because their tunnels have flooded
with rainwater. But soon they go back
into the dark earth.

The Beaver

The beaver makes its home by piling wood and other materials in water. The underwater entrance is hard for enemies to find. The inside stays dry and keeps the beaver family safe. Beavers have special fur that allows them to dry off easily after swimming into their homes.

The May Beetle

This insect spends most of its time above ground. But when the female is ready to lay her eggs, she digs into the earth and leaves the eggs there.

The babies are born underground and then come out into the air when they are strong and ready to fly.

Many different creatures live underground
and in other secret places.

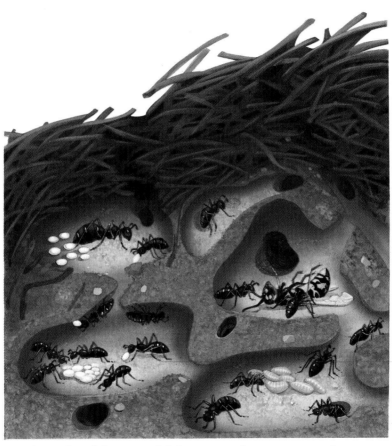

Ants build incredible tunnel systems where
they live and raise their young.

The woodpecker
ses its strong beak
to peck a hole in
he trunk of a tree
for its nest.

The bear goes deep into a cave,
where it is warm and safe in the winter,
spending much of its time sleeping
until spring arrives.

The badger and the fox also live
in caves or dens when they're
not out looking for food.

The mouse finds nuts
and seeds to eat
before it returns to
its underground home.

Titles in the series of
First Discovery Books:

**Airplanes
  and Flying Machines**
All About Time
Bears
Bees
Birds
Boats
Butterflies
The Camera
**Cars and Trucks
  and Other Vehicles**
Castles
Cats
Colors
Construction
Dinosaurs
Dogs
The Earth and Sky
The Egg
Endangered Animals
Fish

Farm Animals
Flowers
Frogs
Fruit
Horses
Houses
The Human Body
**The Ladybug and
  Other Insects**
Light
Monkeys and Apes
Musical Instruments
Night Creatures
Native Americans
Penguins
Pyramids
The Rain Forest
The River
The Seashore
Sports
Trains
The Tree
Turtles and Snails
Under the Ground

Universe
**Vegetables in the
  Garden**
Water
Weather
Whales

Titles in the series of
First Discovery
Atlas Books:

Atlas of Animals
Atlas of Countries
Atlas of the Earth
Atlas of People
Atlas of Plants

Titles in the series of
First Discovery
Hidden World Books:

Under the Ground
Under the Sea

Library of Congress Cataloging-in-Publication Data available.

Originally published in France in 1997 under the title *J'Observe: les animaux sous la terre* by Editions Gallimard Jeunesse.
No part of this publication may be reproduced, or stored in a retrieval system, or transmitted in any form or by any means, electronic, mechanical, photocopying, recording, or otherwise, without written permission of the publisher. For information regarding permission, write to Scholastic Inc., Attention: Permissions Department, 555 Broadway, New York, NY 10012.
ISBN 0-590-43813-1
Copyright © 1997 by Editions Gallimard Jeunesse.
This edition English translation by Wendy Barish. Copyright © 1999 by Scholastic Inc.
This edition American text by Mary Varilla. Copyright © 1999 by Scholastic Inc.
All rights reserved. First published in the U.S.A. in 1999 by Scholastic Inc.
by arrangement with Editions Gallimard Jeunesse, 5 rue Sebastien-Bottin, F-75007, Paris, France.
SCHOLASTIC and A FIRST DISCOVERY BOOK and associated logos are trademarks
and/or registered trademarks of Scholastic Inc.
10 9 8 7 6 5 4 3 2 1   9/9 0/0 01 02 03 04
Printed in Italy by Editoriale Libraria.
First Scholastic printing, March, 1999.